BEING SAFE
IN YOUR
NEIGHBORHOOD

Published by The Child's World®
1980 Lookout Drive • Mankato, MN 56003-1705
800-599-READ • www.childsworld.com

ACKNOWLEDGMENTS
The Child's World®: Mary Berendes, Publishing Director
The Design Lab: Design and production
Red Line Editorial: Editorial direction

LIBRARY OF CONGRESS CATALOGING-IN-PUBLICATION DATA
Kesselring, Susan.
 Being safe in your neighborhood / by Susan Kesselring;
illustrated by Dan McGeehan.
    p. cm.
 Includes bibliographical references and index.
 ISBN 978-1-60954-370-9 (library bound: alk. paper)
1. Safety education–Juvenile literature. 2. Children's accidents–
Prevention–Juvenile literature. 3. Children–Crimes against–
Prevention–Juvenile literature. I. McGeehan, Dan. II. Title.
 HQ770.7.K47 2011
 613.6083–dc22   2010040468

Printed in the United States of America
Mankato, MN
December, 2010
PA02069

About the Author

Susan Kesselring loves children, books, nature, and her family. She teaches K-1 students in a progressive charter school down a little country lane in Castle Rock, Minnesota. She is the mother of five daughters and lives in Apple Valley, Minnesota, with her husband, Rob, and a crazy springer spaniel named Lois Lane.

About the Illustrator

Dan McGeehan spent his younger years as an actor, author, playwright, and editor. Now he spends his days drawing, and he is much happier.

What's fun to do in your neighborhood? Isn't playing with friends great? Do you ever get a sundae at the ice cream shop? Or do you find cool books at the library?

You play in your neighborhood all the time. Learn a few simple rules, and you can have fun and stay safe close to home.

Does your neighborhood have a lot of streets? You know not to play in the street. But what if you need to cross it to get to your friend's house?

Have an adult help you. Find a safe place to cross. You should be able to see far down in both directions. Look both ways for cars. When the coast is clear, walk carefully across the street. Keep your head up and eyes and ears alert for cars.

A crosswalk is a marked path for walkers crossing a road. It is usually marked with white lines on the road. Whenever possible, cross a street at a crosswalk.

6

Are there woods in your neighborhood? Playing in the woods can be fun, but it is easy to get lost among the trees.

A parent will know if it is safe to play in the woods. If it is, stay near the edge of the trees instead of playing deep in the woods. Then you can always find your way out.

When playing in the woods, keep a small flashlight or a whistle in your pocket. When it starts to get dark, you'll be able to see. If you get lost, others can follow the whistle's sound to find you.

It's so fun to watch wild animals in your neighborhood. But avoid feeding squirrels, raccoons, or any other wild guests. Keep your distance, too. These animals need their space.

Stay away from injured and dead animals. Tell an adult about them instead.

If a wild animal bites or scratches you, tell an adult right away. Some animals can give you diseases. You could need to see a doctor.

Do you love to pet dogs? Just remember to always ask the dog's owner first. The dog might not be safe to touch. If the owner says it is okay, let the dog smell you first. Then you can pet the dog gently on its chest or under its chin.

Don't get too close to a dog tied up outside a store or sitting inside a car or a neighbor's yard. The dog doesn't know you. It could get scared and bite you.

If you see a **stray**, you might want to help. But don't get too close to it or try to catch it. Instead, have a parent call the police or an **animal shelter**.

What if a stray dog runs toward you? Don't run away. You should act like a tree. Stare straight ahead and stand very still. If the dog looks like it will bite you, throw something. The dog will chase after what you threw. Then run away as fast as you can.

13

MR. + MRS. JO___S
123 ELM ST.
PH: 555-1234

14

It's possible to lose your parents in a crowd or a store. **Memorize** your address and your parents' phone numbers. Knowing these will help you get home if you are lost.

These numbers might be hard to remember at first, though. While you're learning, write them on a piece of paper. Attach the paper to the inside of your backpack or keep it in your pocket.

It's good to know your parents' full names as well. Then if you get lost, you can explain for whom you are looking.

I ♥ MY NEIGHBORHOOD

Stay where you are when you are lost. Look around for your parents. Call out for them too, even if you are somewhere quiet.

If you still cannot find your parents, tell an adult you are lost. Find a police officer or a worker at a store. Or, find a family and ask one of the parents for help. Before you know it, you will find your parents!

Stores often have speakers to announce things to shoppers. When you are lost, a worker can use the speakers to tell your mom or dad to come meet you.

When you're lost, strangers can help you. But the rules for strangers are different when it's not an **emergency**. If a stranger offers you a ride, candy, or gifts, run away. Go home or to a place with other adults. Never go anywhere with a stranger, even if a stranger says he or she is a friend of your family. And always tell your parents if a stranger bothers you.

Most strangers are good people. But you cannot tell by looking at a person if he or she is someone you can trust.

Always take a friend with you when you are out in the neighborhood. It is safer than going out alone. You can play together and help each other if you have any problems. With a neighborhood buddy, you can stay safe and have fun!

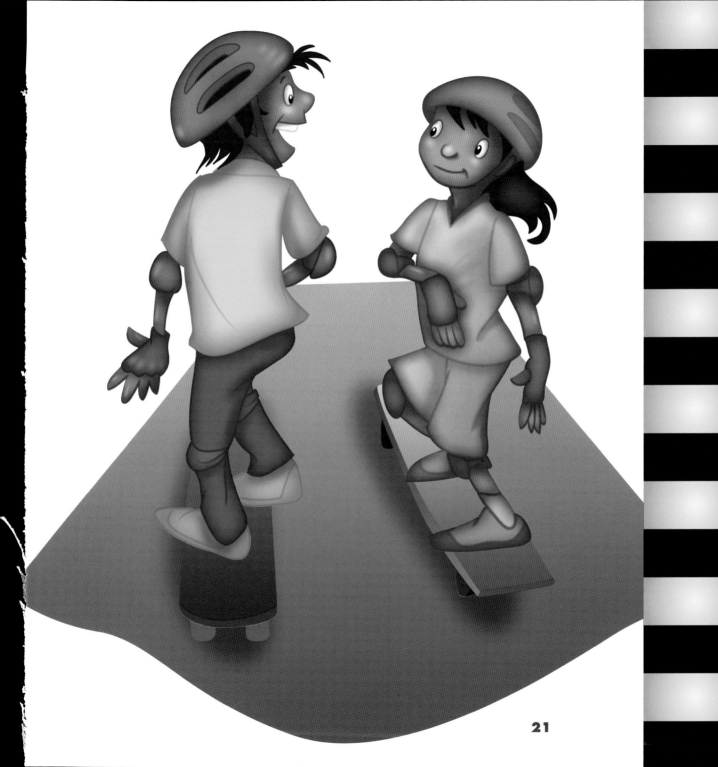

21

NEIGHBORHOOD SAFETY RULES TO REMEMBER

1. Look both ways before crossing the street. Only cross when no cars are coming.

2. Do not get close to wild or stray animals.

3. Always ask before petting a neighbor's dog, cat, or other pet.

4. Do not play in streets or go far into the woods.

5. Learn your phone number, address, and your parents' names and phone numbers.

6. If you are lost, call out for help. Stay where you are, too.

7. Never go anywhere with a stranger.

8. Bring a buddy when you go out in the neighborhood.

Always be safe!

I ♥ MY NEIGHBORHOOD

GLOSSARY

animal shelter (AN-uh-mul SHEL-tur): An animal shelter is a place where lost or unwanted pets stay until they find homes. Have a parent call an animal shelter if you find a stray.

diseases (duh-ZEE-zes): Diseases are kinds of illnesses. Some animals can give people diseases.

emergency (i-MUR-jun-see): An emergency is a sudden situation that needs to be dealt with right away. It's okay to talk to a stranger if it's an emergency.

memorize (MEM-uh-ryz): If you memorize something, you learn it by heart. It's good to memorize your address and parents' full names and phone numbers.

stray (STRAY): A stray is an animal that is lost or has no owner. Do not go close to a stray.

TO LEARN MORE

BOOKS

Joyce, Irma. *Never Talk to Strangers*. New York: Random House, 2009.

Raatma, Lucia. *Safety in Your Neighborhood*. Mankato, MN: Child's World, 2005.

Shore, Diane Z., and Jessica Alexander. *Look Both Ways: A Cautionary Tale*. New York: Bloomsbury, 2005.

WEB SITES

Visit our Web site for links about being safe in your neighborhood: **childsworld.com/links**

Note to Parents, Teachers, and Librarians: We routinely verify our Web links to make sure they are safe and active sites. So encourage your readers to check them out!